Copyright © 2026 VITAL SPARK

THE UNITED STATES
Declaration of Restoration

During her ascent to building a career in movies as an artist, Tessa encountered relentless injustices that qualify her as someone who has by terms outlined in...

The Declaration of Independence

the opportunity...
and
the constitutional duty...

to literally...

do something...

about it.

THIS ISN'T JUST A BOOK. IT'S A SPEECH.
THIS ISN'T JUST A SPEECH. IT'S A DECLARATION.
THIS ISN'T JUST A DECLARATION...

It's the birth of a

founding Mother for America

CONTENT

The Declaration for Restoration 6

Introduction to President 8

America's Invisible Infection 9

New Form of Domestic Violence 11

Pursuing the Impossible 12

Wildfire Nightmares 13

God Joins the 2025 Oscars 15

Crossing the Veil 16

A Founding Mother for America 18

The Hidden Public Health Emergency 20

Funding Salvation Will Save America 22

A Petty Murder sparks More Petty Crime 23

Justice System App Example 24

The Poetry Collection 26

Lawless Media 48

The Perfect Congressman 50

Constitution Updates 51

About the Author 83

THIS SPEECH IS DEDICATED TO:

The Founding Fathers of America

THE UNITED STATES OF AMERICA

The Declaration of Restoration

"We hold these truths to be self-evident, that all men and women are created equal, that they are endowed by their Creator with certain unalienable Rights, that among these are Life, Liberty and the pursuit of Happiness. That to secure these rights, Governments are instituted among Men and Women, deriving their just powers from the consent of the governed —That whenever any Form of Government becomes destructive of these ends, it is the Right of the People to alter or to abolish it, and to institute new Government, laying its foundation on such principles and organizing its powers in such form, as to them shall seem most likely to effect their Safety and Happiness. Prudence, indeed, will dictate that Governments long established should not be changed for light and transient causes; and accordingly all experience hath shewn, that humankind are more disposed to suffer, while evils are sufferable, than to right themselves by abolishing the forms to which they are accustomed. But when a long train of abuses and usurpations, pursuing invariably the same Object evinces a design to reduce them under absolute Despotism, it is their right, it is their duty, to throw off such Government, and to provide new Guards for their future security. — Such has been the patient sufferance of these Colonies; and such is now the necessity which constrains them to alter their former Systems of Government."

The history of a Natural Born American Citizen who performed an especially Meritorious Contribution in a culturally significant Endeavor present in The United States of America is a history met with repeated injuries and usurpations, all having in direct Object the establishment of an absolute Despotism over the Citizen after the performance of an Achievement that has an impact on American history and culture that is likely to be recognized as a major Achievement in the recipient's field long after the Achievement. To prove this, let Facts be submitted to a candid world. Upon being faced with repeated Offenses that rendered her under total and complete Oppression, she Pioneered emerging technology to reinvent a Craft and protect the sanctity of her Virtue while rendering her Country with a Product manufactured in the light of our Creator. Her laborious efforts and pursuit in this unprecedented Mission lasted over half a decade upon which she was restricted to 90% of her time working diligently in total solitude. After many years of trials, failures and tribulations, her Mission achieved success and was met with worldwide critical acclaim.

Yet, despite the Victorious nature of this unprecedented Meritorious Endeavor, she was met with relentless industrial and local government failures. Disregarded and shunned by the very Union formulated to protect her, ignored by Economic Partners, silenced and misrepresented by Industrial Publications, rejected by Agencies created to serve Artisans of her Craft, failed by local Government Policies and Departments, abandoned by Law Enforcement, poisoned by Housing Professionals under contract to protect her, and defrauded by Representatives of the Law. In every stage of these Oppressions she has Petitioned for Redress in the most humble terms: these repeated Petitions have been answered only by repeated Injury. Unruly systemic bodies, whose characters are thus marked by acts that may define an Outlaw, is unfit to be the operational structure of a Free People. It is in turbulent times like these, America would be wise to revisit the words of founding father Thomas Jefferson who said:

"Laws and institutions must go hand in hand with the progress of the human mind. As that becomes more developed, more enlightened, as new discoveries are made, new truths disclosed, and manners and opinions change with the change of circumstances, institutions must advance also, and keep pace with the times. We might as well require a man to wear still the coat which fitted him when a boy, as civilized society to remain ever under the regimen of their barbarous ancestors. It is this preposterous idea which has lately deluged Europe in blood. Their monarchs, instead of wisely yielding to the gradual change of circumstances, of favoring progressive accommodation to progressive improvement, have clung to old abuses, entrenched themselves behind steady habits, and obliged their subjects to seek through blood and violence rash and ruinous innovations, which, had they been referred to the peaceful deliberations and collected wisdom of the nation, would have been put into acceptable and salutary forms. Let us follow no such examples, nor weakly believe that one generation is not as capable as another of taking care of itself, and of ordering its own affairs. Let us, as our sister States have done, avail ourselves of our reason and experience, to correct the crude essays of our first and unexperienced, although wise, virtuous, and well-meaning councils. And lastly, let us provide in our constitution for its revision at stated periods. What these periods should be, nature herself indicates."

This Natural Born American Citizen who achieved this Unprecedented Feat which objectively qualifies for worthy consideration of a Congressional Gold Medal and Presidential Medal of Freedom has informed the offending industrial bodies from time to time of attempts by their own rebellion to extend an unwarrantable jurisdiction over her. She has reminded them of current legislatures and the circumstances of her exemplary achievements.

She has appealed to their native justice and magnanimity, and has requested they disavow these usurpations, which, would inevitably end her life and interrupt her connections and correspondence. They too have been deaf to the voice of justice and of consanguinity. She must, therefore, acquiesce in the necessity, to demand immediate revision in The United States as an operational body with the addition of Industrial Ethics and Business Jurisprudence into the Constitution. And for the support of this Declaration, with a firm reliance on the protection of divine Providence, this Natural Born American Citizen gracefully invites Congress to join in this Endeavor and mutually pledge to each other our Lives, our Fortunes and our sacred Honor.

AN EXCERPT FROM:
THE UNITED STATES OF AMERICA
DECLARATION OF INDEPENDENCE — 1776

"Prudence, indeed, will dictate that Governments long established should not be changed for light and transient causes; and accordingly all experience hath shewn, that mankind are more disposed to suffer, while evils are sufferable, than to right themselves by abolishing the forms to which they are accustomed.

But when a long train of abuses and usurpations, pursuing invariably the same Object evinces a design to reduce them under absolute Despotism, it is their right, it is their duty, to throw off such Government, and to provide new Guards for their future security."

Tessa Lyn:

Mr. President, your recent executive order regarding the city of Los Angeles stated its aim to make communities safer by restoring public order and helping shift people into longer-term institutional treatment since endemic vagrancy, disorderly behavior, sudden confrontations and violent attacks have made our city unsafe." With all due respect, Mr. President, and I'm not stating I am in opposition to this solution, but I am saddened to inform you that this may be a temporary fix... like putting a bandaid on an infected gushing wound that will only get worse with time. Because what's really making our city unsafe... are the causes to homelessness.. one of which is a growing population of unchecked, unregulated American citizens who are turning into criminals that look as harmless as you're everyday grandpa just hanging out on a couch. And I come to you not as a politician but as a natural born American citizen who has fought to survive on the front lines of a broken system. Before I build wealth in Hollywood as an artist, I wanted to know what life is like for the majority of the audiences I will serve with movies and I can sadly say sir... I've experienced firsthand just how dangerous our flawed infrastructures are and how some of them are genuinely set up to deny hardworking innocent Americans their constitutional rights for life, liberty and the pursuit of happiness.

What we are dealing with here Mr. President, besides a catastrophic violation of human rights, is the internal erosion of the American spirit... and I'm not simply talking about a housing crisis. I'm talking about a Public Health Emergency and a silent Civil War... hiding in plain sight. When we take another look at the homeless situation in Los Angeles, let's shift focus to one of the causes to that problem... and to do this I'll share my story... because my story is our story.

Mr. President, in the past three years, I've experienced four illegal evictions back to back for long term lease rentals... and I'm a college graduate who made the Dean's A honor roll list. In fact, I'm a top performer in my field — you just aren't familiar with my work yet because, well, I've also been experiencing delayed recognition by my own industry for over 2 years now (and the reason that is I'll get to in a minute) ...but for now I'll focus on the serial illegal evictions caused by lawless Property Owners who either negligently maintained their building or refused to maintain it at all. These Property Owners, including Real Estate companies and HOAs, are breaking numerous laws and essentially bullying innocent Citizens into homelessness.

Every time I was illegally forced to flee a rental due to its development of an Environmental Hazard, I suffered catastrophic personal property loss to the point where just last summer the only personal items I could keep had to be purified in ammonia. This malicious attack at my foundation put me at risk to becoming homeless, despite me being a hardworking American on track to building a notable career in film... and I'm not alone in this Mr. President. Did you know that right now, in the city of Los Angeles, there are over 4,000 evictions happening each month? From my experience, the percentage of these evictions that are actually legal may only be... 10%. As passionate as you are about keeping our communities safe sir, as you stated this summer during the removal of illegal immigrants, particularly those committed crimes, it is now time to remove the illegal misconduct of lawless Americans.. particular those who are intentionally manipulating an under-regulated industry in order to commit crimes that are forcing hardworking innocent Citizens into homelessness. In my experience, most of the Property Owners doing this.. simply inherited a building then nonchalantly decide to earn money off it, yet, they have no idea how to maintain it. They end up painting over rotten wood which has now become toxic and advertise it as "recently renovated".

This is not only hazardous Mr. President, this is false advertising, fraud, a new form of domestic violence that is damaging to our communities and a domestic attack at Public Health. Essentially what we have here Mr. President is a Civil War between generations. If younger Americans, which make up the majority of renters, can't breath clean air sir, we can't pursue life, liberty or happiness. The way the Rental Industry is currently set up is actively violating America's Constitution.

We have reached the point in history Mr. President when the term "landlord" has finally gotten to people's heads. Property Owners now think they are literal "lords" and act as if they are above the law. Wasn't the term landlord coined during slavery? Aren't we a little overdue to update our language? Speaking of language, just last year shortly after I was asked to comment on my ex being murdered for his catalytic converter, a land "lord" not only failed to repair the water leaks in his ceiling... when I spoke up about the hazardous condition developing in his rental — he blocked my number then sold the building... but not before he ignored two remediation orders by two different companies to instead hire his own "private company" where some guy shows up with what looks like a fake license... [INSERT PHOTO EVIDENCE] Does this organization even exist? I can't find any information about it. So this guy moves a piece of furniture, swabs the carpet underneath then tries to call that an accurate test for the environmental safety condition of the unit... and both of these guys got away with this Mr. President. When I called the police, the LAPD simply drove by and never stopped to take a report. Even the Housing Department failed to address my cry for help. This experience introduced me to a new type of wildfire... an invisible one... that forced me to loose all of my personal property except items that were made out of metal, rock, clay or glass. Once the dumpster was filled... I had to watch fellow Americans ransack my toxic belongings despite the hazardous warning label I put around them. [INSERT MORE PHOTO EVIDENCE]

What we have here Mr. President is a front row seat to view just how bad the current state of your American Rental Industry is; and how the way its currently set up, is feeding a growing population of Americans turning into criminals by taking advantage of an under-regulated industry and using it to maliciously harm our communities and turn ordinary Citizens into barbaric savages.

In the rental before this one, I lived in a condo where the air was also becoming more toxic by the day. Why? ...Because an HOA failed to fix a clogged drain pipe ... and the Property Owner... he hired someone to paint over the resulting water damage instead of repairing it. When I finally discovered the truth, they didn't apologize. They lied. Repeatedly. They tried to convince me it wasn't happening. This is not just dishonesty Mr. President — this is gaslighting — and in psychological terms, gaslighting is not harmless. It's a deliberate attack on someone's mind. Gaslighting Renters into doubting their own reality isn't just unethical...
it's Psychological Violence.

According to the World Health Organization, violence includes any intentional use of power that causes injury, psychological harm, maldevelopment or deprivation. That's exactly what this is Mr. President. It's calculated. It's cruel and its damaging our Communities and the integrity of American soil you're under oath to protect sir. Mr. President, Property Owners manipulating Renters into breathing toxins, while denying the harm, is not just negligence — it's Criminal Assault — and when it happens behind closed doors, under the roof of someone's home, we now have a new form of Domestic Violence. This is more than a housing issue sir. This is a modern day Civil War — happening in silence, behind contracts, leases and rental fees. And Mr. President, this is a direct violation of the safety, dignity, and Constitutional rights of the American people. We're not asking for Rental Industry reform — we are demanding it — demanding protection from a silent epidemic of violence, abuse and neglect.

To make matters worse, this "toxic condo" introduced me to a Lawyer who flips Injured Clients like pancakes... simply to make a quick buck then get on with his next vacation. I caught him coercing with the defense and using calculated tactics to manipulate me into taking a quick settlement. I even had to write our first mediation brief myself since his version was like a paper thin version of Swiss cheese. To top it off, he hired a Mediator who refused to look at any factual evidence with has a 100% track record of siding with the defense. Isn't it true that unanimously siding with one side mean the person is inserting personal bias into our justice system? Aren't the words "bias" and "judge" opposites? What is that oath again? Oh, yeah... 28 U.S. Code § 453... which states:

> "I, ____ , do solemnly swear that I will administer justice without respect to persons, and do equal right to the poor and to the rich, and that I will faithfully and impartially discharge and perform all the duties incumbent upon me as a (insert judge title) under the Constitution and laws of The United States. So help me God."

Well, look at that! "So help me God.' Now seems like a pretty good time for God to step in because the fact The United States of America is becoming a nation where people get away with violating their oaths ... means American soil is truly rotting sir. This type of behavior is a betrayal to our country... which feels like a new form of treason. Maybe we can get an AI-assisted justice system to help weed out the toxicity that's turning America into a country running an "injustice system."

*— and trust me, Mr. President—
I wish I could stop here but life on the front lines of America gets even worse...*

Let's fast forward from 2022 to 2025 to rental number three. The third long term lease rental in the three year illegal eviction spree. Turns out this billionaire Property Owner is running a massive slumlord operation all across the city of Los Angeles. Talk about a growing homeless population.. this guy has a direct hand feeding it. He creates LLCs for Real Estate companies that prohibit Renters from having any way to contact them. All communication is funneled through a "Building Manager" who is trained to bully and harass tenants into submission in the form of denying responsibility, disturbing the peace and threatening three day eviction notices left and right while his company subtly and steadily breaks laws. It seems the Building Manager may not even be aware she's using psychological warfare tactics to subconsciously deteriorate a Renter's self esteem to coerce them into a state of submission as she attempts to exploit illicit rent payments.

I'll explain — when I reminded this Building Manager the Owner still needs to reimburse what he legally owes in temporary displacement damages… instead of responding to my many communication attempts to work out a reimbursement method… the entire complex suddenly gets toilet seat upgrades. Would you call this reckless spending? Irresponsible budgeting? Or just a passive aggressive way of insulting me? Check it out… even the toilet brand they chose seems suspiciously manipulative.

Well.. you know what I'm not going to flush down the toilet Mr. President… the production company Vital Spark. Did you know you're actually looking at The American who has achieved what is said to be the World's Largest Performance by a Motion Picture Artist in Human History? I may have set up to six world records that are waiting for certification for over 2 years now. The 5 1/2 years before that, I spent 90% of my time in solitude learning and executing essentially every aspect of filmmaking from pre-production, production and post-production to craft the first ever feature film fundamentally made by hand… all before the emergence of AI. It's called Cinema Rebel... and it went on to receive 18 awards and nominations at festivals worldwide, getting thousands of festival invites before it was roadblocked by major festivals who refused to watch it, industry publications who refused to report about it, Guinness World Records who said the new records would take too much work to verify… even my own Union hung up on me and refused to work out a new contract. I'm technically one of the first people on planet Earth to ever explore the cinematic capabilities of an iPhone and am said to be the first female to ever make a feature film with it… but you have to dig deep to find out the truth about this unprecedented accomplishment in film. Why? …maybe systemic oppression? Gender inequality? Industrial betrayal? Even google's AI has been missing the most important facts about me — which is essential to reporting about film history accurately.

…but let's circle back quickly to the Rental Industry because we're missing an important element here: Short Term Rental Apps. Mr. President, you announced a gold rush coming soon. Well, I'll tell you what's rushing your way right now… another golden nugget of truth. Your beloved Rental Apps are false advertising left and right. They've been withholding funds from wildfire victims and facilitating a platform that permits toxic tort, sexual predators, bullying, harassment… even price gouging after a natural disaster. I'll prove it — let's jump to January 2025 during the Southern California wildfires. Blazing fires in the Pacific Palisades by the coast. Fires raging in the valleys. Flames approaching all around me. Smoke and toxic air circling me like a wolf pack. I go outside and see flames from the Sunset Fire approaching my building…

I literally just rebuilt my life from total destruction for the second time in two years so I pack up as much as I could… definitely the hard drives that are evidence to the new records for filmmaking and movie props that are now one-of-a-kind artifacts. I whip together a cargo rack on the roof of a car and head straight to the nearest body of water away from the fires.. the Salton Sea.

Knowing nothing about the Salton Sea or Bombay Beach (except for what was listed on the rental ad), after I jam packed the white BMW i3, I hit the road.

An hour or so into the drive (after I luckily survived an interaction with a semi-truck driving serial killer who tried to run me off the road) I do more research on Bombay Beach. I discover this lil' town was popping back in the 50's. A big celebrity hotspot for people like Frank Sinatra and the Beach Boys. I get excited to check it out — until I realize I was leaving toxic air to head straight into even more toxic air. Apparently this Rental App doesn't fact or safety check any of their listings. As it turns out, the Salton Sea is one of the most polluted bodies of water in the entire country!

I obviously canceled that reservation but didn't feel comfortable leaving this loaded car exposed in a hotel parking lot so I slept in it that night. The next day, I settled into a Rental with a garage.. thinking "Peace, at last!" Nope. Straight back into the car. Why? …because apparently these Property Owners have no idea what a dishwasher leak looks like. Well, here ya go… [INSERT PHOTO EVIDENCE]

It's subtle, yet, it's not. This is called… "wet wood"… and it grows mold, mildew and all sorts of things that spread spores .01 microns in size which are essentially invisible to the human eye. Not only that.. the bathrooms there failed to comply with Building Safety Codes of having a mechanical fan.. which due to the musty smell means behind the paint is a simmering stew of wood rot.

Ladies and Gentleman… I'm going to have to burst your bubble here… specifically the one in your "bath… room"… It has been discovered a mechanical fan in every bathroom with a shower is mandatory, and must run on average for 30 minutes after every shower. Why? To protect the integrity of your home. Moisture rots building materials… especially wood… its guaranteed.. only a matter of time … and during that time… the damage it does, includes your body. So, as I pack up my things and book a new Rental.. of course this Property Owner does the same thing as the other ones.. lie about the water damage then try to bully me so they can steal my money. Meanwhile, the Rental App is allowing all of this to happen. Yup — never got the money back and didn't spend a single night there. When I finally get to the next Rental… looking forward to a good nights sleep… things get even worse.

After I got out of the shower, it felt as if I was being watched. Then I noticed almost all of the windows were missing curtains. I spotted weird electrical wires installed all over the house… with little lights coming from wall switches.. even the shower head in the master bathroom had a light in it but the other bathroom shower head didn't. I started to hear creeks coming from the ceiling above me. It sounded like people were in the attic. I tried to ignore it to get some sleep.. but a few hours later… it wasn't my alarm that woke me up… [INSERT VIDEO EVIDENCE] I thought maybe it was a drain pipe.. or the pool pump. So I check and go outside. Nope — the pool pump was outside. Then all of a sudden… [INSERT VIDEO EVIDENCE] So I called the police… but apparently they don't have enough funding to bring spy camera detection tools (or go check the attic) so they just left me there. I was so exhausted from moving around so much that I took my chances and… got lucky. I survived the night and checked out the next morning — but right before I left — that's when I caught 'em… changing the tempo just enough to make it very clear… this was not a pipe.

Mr. President, I'm not sure if you're familiar with the term "frogging" or "sexual predators." Well, in the new U.S. Rental Safety Department, we'll need to have all Rental App listings with a "Certified Safe" badge to confirm these Rentals abide by the law, are up to Building Safety Codes, in a sanitary, habitable condition.. free from water damage, spyware and predator activity… because Mr. President, this story gets even worse. As I check into the next Rental, now in Palm Springs (since the fires were still blazing around LA) I noticed a few things somewhat troublesome but tried to make the most of it — until I opened a pantry then VIOLA … *future organ failure ala mode.* [INSERT PHOTO EVIDENCE] I finally cave and check into a Hotel to take my chances parking the loaded car with valet.

negligence and gaslighting in attempting to get out of their legal responsibilities to provide clean and sanitary conditions

To not repair water damage materials is against the law

^^ health code violation ^^

Code (CBC) regulate water damage in building materials. These codes state that water-damaged building materials should be replaced or

Meanwhile, I bet you can guess what the Rental App and the Property Owner did? The same exact thing … lied about the water damage then try to bully me to keep the money, without me ever staying a single night there.

Mr. President, let's be crystal clear— if a Property Owner accepts payment from a Renter.. this means.. they work for the Renter! It's not the other way around. Property Owners are providing a service, and as such, they need to be trained on how to legally and ethically provide that service. Property Owners are now, in my experience, unanimously overstepping their power, abusing their freedoms and turning into criminals. This is literally American Citizens intentionally attacking other American Citizens — on a grand scale — Real Estate companies, HOAs, Rental Apps.. breaking multiple laws and assaulting Citizens.

THIS IS A SILENT CIVIL WAR MR. PRESIDENT
AND AN INDUSTRIAL MOCKERY TO LAW AND ORDER IN THIS COUNTRY

Before I wrap this up, let's briefly jump to February 2025… because I'm afraid Mr. President… the silent Civil War that is the current state of the American Rental Industry continues. After the chronic relocations during this wildfire evacuation period, as a result of the relentless offenses of the Rental App and lawless Property Owners… as you can imagine I fell behind schedule in launching Vital Spark's debut movie slate. When I was finally able to return to LA after the fires died down, besides being greeted with a mudslide warning, I noticed a crack had developed on an exterior wall directly connected to my long term lease Rental. Knowing exactly what that would lead too — I informed the Building Manager and requested the crack be sealed immediately before rain water got inside.. which would cause the internal materials to become wet..

which would lead to wood rot.. that would spread through building like an infestation… because that's what it is! But of course, she has no license. No credentials. No idea what she's doing.. she can barely look me straight in the eye in fact. She mocks me then laughs off my concern. A week or two goes by, then I notice she had someone paint over the crack… with normal paint… but not after… we had a series of rainy days sir.

Mr. President, before I explain how this story gets even worse, you see, God showed up. As if by magic — either the movie title, plot or theme from all 10 Oscar nominated films for Best Picture this year seamlessly tell my story!   …and SPOILER ALERT… the final film in the puzzle is titled "I'm Still Here." So, as Vital Spark and I hustle to put a tribute film together for Oscar season, the air in the third long term lease Rental takes a straight nosedive in quality, forcing me to flee for safety yet again. At this point, my hope was dwindling. After working overtime in solitude for 5 1/2 years to accomplish something unprecedented in film to then be consistently discarded and violated by fellow Americans and the systems put in place which claim to protect my alienable rights to life, liberty and the pursuit of happiness… as you can imagine.. my faith in people and in this planet was hanging on by a thread. Not to mention the physical exhaustion of having to move and relocate Vital Spark's office which included computer equipment, monitors.. hard drives, cables, cords, microphones… lights, laptops, notebooks, books… I needed something to inspire me. A jetliner view, sir. You can appreciate this. You, yourself, have very fine taste in Real Estate.

In hoping the Rental App would finally make up for their repetitive transgressions earlier that year, I clicked on the App and searched for the next Rental. As I did, a voice inside told me to do something different this time — which lead me removing the usual search filters to check out everything available in the area. Hollywood Hills, Beverly Hills, Bel Air… I started to see listings go for 50, 60, 80 thousand a night. I flipped through their photos. They were stunning. Some of them a little too stunning. Almost as if they weren't real. Then I got an eerie feeling in the pit of my stomach. You know that feeling you get when something just isn't right? Suddenly, I started to see blood splashing all over the walls of the gorgeous rooms in the photos. Then the dollar amounts on the ads started turning into how many gallons of blood it cost the Property Owner to get the estate. It felt as if… after surviving so many rotten Rentals and seeing how the souls of their Owners were rotten too.. I was beginning to see behind a veil of reality for the first time. The invisible realm of truth… but instead of seeing invisible mold spores.. I was seeing the invisible blood shed that is plaguing America.

Then, viola. An ad pops up with "jetliner" in the title. I checked it out. It looked perfect.. I loved the jaguar sculpture… may even be the best view in the city. It felt a lil' heavy on the pocket in that moment though so I kept scrolling. Til I stumbled on another ad that also had "jetliner" in the title. The girl in the photos looked just like me.. and there was even a teddy bear like the Cinema Rebel movie poster! So, I booked it, then packed up the office to rush off and edit the Oscar tribute film.

Before I go further Mr. President I'll just say… if I ever doubted my beliefs in God… this next experience solidified them.

When I arrived at the next rental — the first thing I noticed was an odd design on the decor pillows in the living room. [INSERT PHOTO EVIDENCE] They looked like fangs.. made me feel a little uneasy so I tossed them in a closet and continued settling in. When I got to the master bedroom, a large painting also stuck out to me as odd. I never imagined we'd be having this conversation (and sadly I didn't take a clear photo of it) so I drew it for you. Peculiar, to say the least.

What's even more peculiar is that despite my best efforts after relocating the office to dive into the film edit, over the next two days my ability to think and function was on a steady decline. I had no idea why.. until one afternoon, after parking the car in an outdoor parking area, I look up and boom. [INSERT PHOTO EVIDENCE]

Talk about invisible poison — this was staring at me right in the face. Apparently, these Property Owners also have no idea how to maintain their building. Or they simply don't care. I started to wonder if the rest of the house was rotting too. As I looked closer… I bet you can guess what I found.. but of course… the classic "renovation" technique — just paint over water damage and no one will know! Oh wait, they forgot these… [INSERT MORE PHOTO EVIDENCE] Maybe they figured no one will look up. Well, I'm looking up Mr. President, and I'm not letting another lazy American who's now turning Criminal (and these many Rental App grievances) interfere with the launch of Vital Spark.

Did you know that our content is actually curated to improve the lives of the audience... which includes fellow American citizens and I know you can respect that. So, knowing water damaged buildings get more dangerous at night (because at night wood rot breathes and their spores increase in number) I ordered a tent to sleep inside the 'tent-shaped' Rental to continue working and hit the deadline. But, you can imagine, that didn't go very well... so I began searching for a new Rental. Before I did, I pulled up the first listing with "jetliner" in the title and spotted a stuffed tiger in one of its photos. I began to wonder if I was meant to go there the entire time. A tiger is my high school mascot. I believe your mascot was a Black Knight, Mr. President? Well, this black night was sleepless to say the least. I couldn't get over the lingering suspicion that I somehow got tricked into being here ... so I took a chance and booked the first choice "jetliner" Rental for a check-in the next day. In the morning, after I informed the Property Owners of the tent-shaped Rental and the dangerous conditions in their property, I was given another blow of Psychological Violence... the ol' "gaslighting" assault... just lie about.. deny it... try to make me question reality... no one will know! Speaking of "no one will know" — Mr. President, I'm sure you've heard of the term Serial Killer?

Well, here's where this story picks up speed. As I'm arguing with this new Property Owner, refusing to be poisoned against my will... yet again... because after all... forcing someone to breathe toxic air is not only a violation of their Constitutional rights... it can technically fall under the definition of torture! And, of course, my torture continued as the cat named Bullseye snuck outside and bolted under the house. When I climbed down to get him, I noticed scattered soda cans and water bottles under the deck. Then I saw an active water leak right next to electrical wires ... here we have another hazard... and this one could set the entire property on fire ... just sitting there right in front of me! Meanwhile... of course... Bullseye was not right in front of me — so I had to crawl in deeper.

As I continued to search for him, now crawling around on my hands and knees like a human version of a leopard, I found a disturbing collection of broken porcelain dolls wrapped in Saran wrap. They were shattered to pieces yet held together by the plastic. I looked around and couldn't find any other belongings to resemble an abandoned family storage area. Then I noticed how much space there was to crawl down there. I began to get a feeling there may be body parts buried there. I wanted to find out but I didn't have on the proper gear to keep crawling so I returned to the staircase. As I crawled back toward the staircase, I noticed a sculpture of a Virgin Mary laid out on the grass then I looked over and saw a similar sculpture of a Virgin Mary propped up perfectly straight — that's when my stomach dropped. I realized I may actually be surrounded by the presence of real evil... but instead of breaking down, I figured, "Well, if the Devil is real.. that means God is too." So I start praying. I prayed for Bullseye to return to me... and what do ya know...he appeared.

Right there by the staircase. When I picked him up to hug him… he just snapped… like a light switch. It wasn't him anymore. It seemed like he literally got possessed while he was exploring down there… but knowing the real (the sweet) him, I took him inside and locked him in a room til we were ready to relocate all over again.

> *Mr. President, whether or not there are human remains buried down there.. and whether or not Bullseye really did get possessed by a demon or the Devil himself.. the fact is.. this is The United States of America.. the land of the free.. not the land of the free to harm or kill whomever you want.*

America was founded on the principle of loving our neighbors as ourselves. Not poisoning our neighbors against their will to then manipulate them into believing the poison never existed. This is beyond a civil offense Mr. President. It's criminal and a direct violation of the principles this Country was founded on. In fact, here's a refresher:

> *"We hold these truths to be self-evident, that all men are created equal, that they are endowed by their Creator with certain unalienable Rights, that among these are Life, Liberty and the pursuit of Happiness.— That to secure these rights, Governments are instituted, deriving their just powers from the consent of the governed, --That whenever any Form of Government becomes destructive of these ends, it is the Right of the People to alter or to abolish it, and to institute new Government, laying its foundation on such principles and organizing its powers in such form, as to them shall seem most likely to effect their Safety and Happiness."*

Mr. President, painting over toxic building materials then calling it "renovation" is like a farmer taking spoiled milk, tossing in some dirt then labeling it as "recently remodeled luxury chocolate."

> *It is tragic our country has reached a point in history where rental property signs are more accurate to say "Now Torturing" instead of "Now Leasing."*

This is a colossal failure in the eyes of the Founding Fathers of America, Mr. President. In fact, does America have a Founding Mother yet? Well, it does now. And she's demanding nationwide reform requiring all Property Owners (for both long and short term Rentals… both commercial and residential) to be licensed, monitored and regulated so we can ensure they're all operating safely and securely.

If anyone wants to receive income from leasing a property in America, the Rental needs to be safe, hazard free and predator free… just like how we require a barber to have a license to cut the hair on our heads. It's now time to require a Property Owner to have a license to put a roof over our heads.

In addition to being licensed, Short Term Rentals Apps need to have a "Certified Safe" badge on listings in order to be eligible to operate in The United States. Here's the vision and it's not complicated — we do it like we do for restaurants. We have a Health Department Inspector execute an unannounced Inspection using the latest tools and equipment to verify there are no safety hazards, substandard building conditions, spyware or illicit activity. They have private access to the booking schedules and perform randomized Inspections during the cleaning transition period in-between guest check-ins and check-outs. Any violations found will be documented given an allotted time for correction. Repeat offenders will lose their license and become ineligible to earn income off the property til they earn their license back. Furthermore, we must begin prosecuting the criminal misconduct of Property Owners. No one is above the law, Mr. President.

You fight for law and order, sir — well, this means we need you to address the causes to homelessness — as well as the homeless themselves. Otherwise it's discriminatory. Property Owners who willfully and consistently false advertise their listings and intentionally expose Renters to potentially deadly pathogens is a silent yet calculated Civil War and an abomination to this nation sir.

— And here's where the public health emergency hiding-in-plain-sight comes in —

We have now reached a point in our Nation's history were enough time has passed for the majority of our buildings to have either decayed due to weather, suffered micro cracks due to platonic shifts, have construction defects or outdated building materials. American is now both literally and metaphorically (and sadly spiritually) rotting beneath our feet and all around us. Right now it's estimated around 75% of our buildings have some form of water damage… and for the majority of these… it's hidden. Which means — around 235 million Americans are currently being exposed to potentially deadly pathogens and most have no idea! What's even worse … according to recent studies around 25% of humans are born without the genetic makeup required to develop a proper immune system response to these pathogens. Which means — around 65 million Americans are currently at-risk for developing rapid on-set disease because of this! And look… I get it… preventing wood rot is hard. I even bet certain rooms in The Whitehouse are compromised by now --

But this is 2025 people... We have the technology. We have the knowledge.

IT'S TIME TO CLEAN AMERICA

Here's what I suggest we do Mr. President:

1) Develop a Vaccine for the 25% of humanity born with a genetic predisposition for a hyper-immune response to these pathogens (HLA-DR / HLA-DQ) and share this discovery with other countries to aid in our world peace efforts.

2) Order a mandatory nationwide language update and replace "landlord" with "Property Owner" on all contracts, leases, websites, documents… effective immediately.

3) Establish a new board for the Rental Industry to ensure Property Owners who lease their properties for compensation (either commercially or residentially) have the necessary licenses, training, skills and knowledge to operate safely and professionally.

4) Establish and mandate new construction methods and materials — that help immunize wood to water. Regulate AI drone inspections during constructions and tax violators until they are in compliance.

5) Work with AI — to develop a tool that can detect hidden water damage and mildew growth without cutting open a wall. Simultaneously, work with AI to create an LED light system or something similar to put inside walls — the idea is to be able to flip a switch at night before bed and run an internal wall disinfection process that operates regularly. Note on this * we'll need to establish a fire hazard prevention method along with it.

6) Require all Remediators — to be licensed, monitored and regulated. Tax violators until they are in compliance.

7) Update our Medical System — to train doctors (particularly PCP doctors) on water damaged building / mycotoxin exposure; along with establishing an insurance-covered recovery protocol.

8) Nationwide Education — for both Owners and Renters on proper ventilation and maintenance practices. Example: protocols for checking conditions behind dishwashers and washing machines. If we can update the manufacturing blueprint of these machines to aid in this, that will help. For example— require they be built on a floor sliding track to be easily pulled out of position so the owner/renter can check surrounding building materials periodically.

9) Establish the safety exposure limit to this pathogen.. if it's 0 then it's 0.. and we face what we have to face, united, as a country.

10) Online Clean Up — remove outdated articles that contain inaccurate information. Articles on health and safety matters need to be accurate, current or otherwise labeled "contains false, outdated information."

By the way, Mr. President —

You recently mentioned you may "defund" Los Angeles because you believe L.A. is failing to do enough enforcement. Well, here's another solution for you... in fact, you may LOVE this one because it can also help pay off America's debt!

We create a nationwide Criminal Tax Law that utilizes the harmful actions of lawless Americans to pay down our nation's debt through an immediate Crime Tax. This will make both our cities online and on land more safe. Plus, it will improve the value of the American dollar. When we develop a new AI-assisted justice system (which will include an App) we can revolutionize crime reporting and not only help restore law and order in this country (by increasing the speed and efficiency of crime and civil offense reporting) we will help prevent the collapse of the American dollar, steer off the weaponization of AI and help keep food on the tables and medicines in the cabinets of lower income families. With all the warnings we are getting daily, we don't have time to waste here. We need to jump on this immediately and see what we can create since time is of the essence.

Here's how it could work:

Let's take the article by The New York Post for example titled *"'General Hospital' star Johnny Wactor's family doesn't want his ex-fiancée Tessa Farrell speaking on LA murder"* First of all, this reads like an attempt to bully a person out of their First Amendment right to freedom of speech by the use of threats/intimidation in order to passive-aggressively rob them of their voice... which ummm... is illegal.

So, we first upload a screenshot of this article, along with a link to it into the App Let's call the App "HONOR," for example. We then report the suspicion of a First Amendment rights violation and possible Defamation. We would upload evidence to prove how the article failed to include pertinent information such as his family was telling reporters a different version of the events surrounding the murder. Specifically stating "Johnny did not confront the men or try to stop them, but they shot him anyway." We would then upload clips showing how I was informing the reporters Johnny shielded his co-worker and verbally addressed the crime during the act. HONOR would then begin to conceptualize the likelihood Johnny's family developed negative feelings around the experience of having a different version of events exposed publicly but would likely request more information.

To assist further, I would then upload screenshots of sections in the article that shift focus away from the LA murder and onto my personal character and credibility. I would need to explain and prove how there was no character or credibility evaluation done because no one (neither a reporting journalist or commenters in the article) ever inquired about any of the facts surrounding my interviews nor did they educate themselves on any of the facts related to my past or current life circumstances. For example, an adequate character and credibility analysis may begin with a question like "Did I reach out to press myself?" The answer is no. So to prove this — I would upload interview requests I received along with screenshots of the many attempts I took to connect with his family prior to interviewing.

I would then upload screenshots of text messages with a friend showing how I did not want to interview about the murder of someone I cared about but was doing so out of pressure I received from other people, circumstantial obligation I felt to help his legacy become more than a crime victim while upholding a long-held goal of mine to improve the safety of our communities. To provide evidence for this, I would upload additional texts and emails along with feature film scripts I've written (which all have endings designed to improve humanity) to show that I was already passionate about improving the safety of our communities prior to Johnny's murder. However, since those scripts were not publicly accessible, HONOR would likely request more information.

I would then upload evidence to prove that, at that time, I had already earned unprecedented achievements in film and specifically mention the six new world record titles pending certification at Guinness. To prove status as a public figure and top performer in the field of film acting, I would include links to my performer profiles along with the Inventor's Digest Cover, American Reporter, USA Reformer, Broadway World magazine articles. I would specify in the comment section how all of this information was publicly accessible at the time, both on the internet, the websites of these publications, my professional website and on social media. HONOR would begin to calculate this is likely to be a case of Defamation due to the "reckless disregard for the truth," and note how the NY Post deliberately ignored all contradictory evidence and failed to fact check prior to publishing unverified claims through a potentially biased source.

While spotlighting an accusation in an article that claimed I was "clout clashing," HONOR may suspect an act of malice with intent to cause harm from another "purposeful avoidance of the truth" due to the lack of reciprocated communication, zero effort to obtain knowledge or understanding of the facts surrounding my interviews, and a failure to acknowledge career accomplishments at that time. HONOR may likely suspect it also to be a case of discrimination based on gender and may begin inquiring on the justice I would be seeking. For example, HONOR may ask if I'd like to press charges. In this instance, given the fact the person responsible for the defamatory statements recently lost a child, I would chose to decline and serve as a channel for their anger to help them grieve. I'll explain this further in just a minute — but first — let's point out how the criminals responsible were all 18 year old gang members. Did you know that, sir? Why is no one talking about how we basically lost 5 lives that day? These boys will never live a normal, healthy life. The root problem here is: What is causing people, particularly adolescents, to commit crimes. Is it video games? Is it poverty? Is it crimes forcing other people to enter poverty so that turning to crime becomes a means for survival? Or is it simply because crime is contagious.. and so much so that it's contagious biologically, socially, spiritually… even through physics. I'll explain:

1) Crime can be contagious through PHYSICS — When my ex's family received news of my his murder, this was like a blunt force trauma blow of energy to. A person's natural survival instinct in a moment like this is to immediately reduce the level of impact… and a simple way to do this is to keep the energy in motion. So, by launching an attack at me… my credibility and reputation… since it's common knowledge an act like that is likely to cause someone to feel pain—- the blunt force energy was kept in motion… and redirected at me. 26
2) Crime is contagious through BIOLOGY — Once the experience of a "petty crime" became a reality for Johnny's family, another common survival instinct of the brain is to find or create another reality of "petty crime" to prevent the brain from entering a state of cognitive dissonance. Cognitive dissonance creates extreme discomfort in the brain. Since they were already experiencing pain from the tragic news, reducing brain tension was essential for coping.
3) Crime is contagious SPIRITUALLY — When someone experiences this level of pain, their spirit becomes vulnerable due to entering a weakened state. In this case, the reporting journalists who speculated about my intentions during interviews, instead of doing factual research, they applied pressure to Johnny's family through means of gossip instead of formal investigation — since they were more likely to go along with casual agreement over formal accuracy due to being in a weakened state. This would, in turn, increase the likelihood that there would be drama and publication circulation.
4) Crime is contagious through SOCIOLOGY — As humans, we are hardwired to be communal beings. We thrive in a community. When we know someone else is in pain, our pain is reduced by no longer feeling alone in that emotion. This is a subconscious way of soothing ourselves and a subtle way to connect with others by means of sharing a joint emotional experience.

I'm sure you've heard of the term 'hurt people, hurt people'? Well, suffice it to say, America's media personnel need to be properly educated on all of this so we don't allow crime to perpetuate and swirl around society like a whirlpool. The American media has a legal responsibility to uphold the integrity of their position as our source of news... not perpetuators of criminal misconduct.. and I'm afraid sir... it gets worse...

While still in the HONOR app, I would next upload a clip showing how the NY Post edited out a section of my video to materially change the meaning of the words in their article. Specifically, when I stated "I haven't spoken to him in a few years. I've been busy making my movie and he always distracted me." They deliberately removed this portion of my video in order to then publish an article stating "Johnny's Mom said they haven't spoken in 2-3 years." Upon this discovery, HONOR may begin to suspect an alteration of evidence — which is a federal crime 18 U.S. Code § 35 — where they willfully and maliciously imparted false information with reckless disregard for human life due to the article's intent to damage and eliminate a person's credibility, regardless of (and without ever acknowledging) contradictory factual evidence. HONOR would begin to calculate a Crime Tax Fine based on this information, which would likely increase as I upload a screenshot of the reporting journalist stating further false information. Specifically: "Farrell has since created a Youtube account to which she uploaded her tearful video."

I would upload a screenshot of the publicly accessible Youtube Profile showing the channel was in fact created several years prior to 2024. HONOR would incorporate a new offense and likely conclude the reporting journalist to be publishing articles with a "reckless disregard for the truth" and a "purposeful avoidance of the truth" due to these consistent failures to fact check prior to publishing. HONOR may ask if I wish to add further comments or information. In this instance, I would, since it's common protocol to analyze a person's values while assessing their character and credibility. To provide evidence to support this, I would upload a poetry collection that was publicly visible on my Instagram at the time since poetry gives the reader an insight into an author's values, personality and character traits.

While we're at it Mr. President —
Let's quickly revisit these shall we...

POEM 1: FEBRUARY 26, 2023

[Untitled]

Out of the ash
Arose a city of angels
Out of the ruins
Comes a community for the kingdom of good

Only after one knows the taste of defeat
After their palate is calibrated to know loss
May the human spirit rise into everlasting victory

For it is in the aftermath of loss that…
One may discover their deepest self
One may discover their present limits
Because… it is in a moment of loss we are presented with a choice
To surpass our limits or stay down

And if we chose to rise
Out of the ash
Up into the sun
No matter how difficult
No matter how taxing
No matter how painful

We have become a beacon of light
So bright it blinds the dark
So beautiful
So courageous
Evil can't fight back

Because angel warriors of light know…
The only think evil needs to flourish…
Is for good people to stand by and do nothing

The time has come
To rise out of the mud
To take the everlasting victory
And brighten our world… again

POEM 2: MARCH 25, 2023

"We Out Here"

What does it mean

When someone says be yourself?

What if

You don't know who that is

And if you don't

How do you find out?

Maybe life is a series of circumstances

And who we are

Is created by how we handle them

So then

If we don't know who we are

Maybe that means

We aren't consciously living

Maybe that means

We're controlled by our circumstances

Maybe that means

We're stuck in a reactive state of mind

Floating by week by week

Never giving ourselves

The chance

The honor

The luxury

To know who we are

So then, instead of reacting to life

What if, we pause to think

We think about

Who we want to be

Who we dream of becoming

We can now imagine

How that person would respond to our circumstances

Then suddenly

A series of steps brightens before our feet

And as we take each step

We are gifted the privilege of knowing who we are

But we only receive that gift

When we no longer stay a passenger in our life

When we become a co-captain with the universe/God

Because only it/he/she/they take part in…

The things out of our control

In our life... our circumstances

So now

Who we are seems to be our decisions

Who we are seems to be in our control

When we take life into our hands

When we get out here... in life

We receive the ultimate gift

Of knowing ourselves

POEM 3: APRIL 8, 2023

"Growing Up"

*Heavy, dirty, messy
The pain of growth*

*Comes in many forms
Icky, sticky, nasty*

*What's good for us...
Sometimes... worms*

*Worms eat away at what's
dead, rotten, unclean*

*Our instinct...
Resist, deny and kill them*

But what if...

Instead of resisting worms

*We thank them
We thank them... for making clear what needs to be ridden*

*And Growth?
Growing up...
The active participation in expanding one's sense of self*

*One's experience of reality
One's realm of existence*

Which makes a worm... a sign of rot and death

*We... embrace their presence
We... feed the worms and move on*

*We move on to... what's pure
What's raw, clean, alive*

We understand... when we have worms
Which may come in the form of...

A toxic friend
An ending relationship
A budding enemy
A challenger
Doubter
Expanding Obstacle
Never-ending negative circumstance

We take it as...

The gift of information
A gift
Informing us... there's something within
Ourselves, our life...
That must be killed

And the presence of a worm...
A sign... it's time to let go
We let go... to let live

So we celebrate the worms
We allow them to feast
And when their meal is done.. finished.. complete

We ban them
For worms are... gluttonous, greedy, lustful
Worms are not created to feast on pure and clean

And it's our job to inform them
When it's time to stop

When we... order the worms to leave
So we can live a pure, clean life
That's the moment we've...

Grown Up

 **tessafarrellxo**
♫ Seven Lions · Falling Away (feat. Lights)

POEM 3: JUNE 2, 2023
[untitled]

Break me open
Take a microscope to my insides
Are they rotten
Or are they alive

Is there purity in my veins
Or conformity chains

This world in a
Constant state of pain
Yet things never stay the same

A rate race for one piece of cheese
People killing each other on the way with ease

Why is authenticity so rare
Why is truth buried

Why can't people live in peace
Why can't people stay married

Where is safe
Where is home
Everywhere we turn
Darkness roams

Despite this I...

I still believe in the light
Even with the fog in my windshield
I still believe in love

Even though my innocence they tried to kill

Despite everything I...

Have hope above all else

Hang faith on all my shelves

And when it's time to go to sleep

I will dream of the world I want this to be

A world where we all get along

A world where the light set us free

POEM 4: OCTOBER 10, 2023

God unlock our mouths
Bless them with the fruit of the spirit

Fill them only with light
With love

Scream it loud... make them hear it...

The words that make a soul elevate
The energy of life... love...
...what makes this planet populate

People got lost in the seas of confusion
Tackled by waves of submersion

As darkness thrusted flawed ideals upon them daily
While temptation and comparison drove them crazy

And... our innocence...
Evil tried to bend and break
Yet what it wants.. we won't let it take..

Because we're stepping up and we will protect...

Protect ourselves
Our hearts
Our soul

For we have the power to kill demons
Evaporate darkness and form a new rule

A family of divine light
Carefully created for one another
Who long to live right
Live just
Live strong with each other

Our balance is key... to what makes us strong

As we create in unity
Beauty that births the melodies
For our next songs

POEM 6: JUNE 24, 2024

"A Real Smile"

What makes a smile real?

Is it the breath behind it?
Or the eyes above it?

Is it in the mind?
Or in the soul?

Is it simply a feeling within our control?

And when life brings us pain...

When there's nothing we could possibly gain...

And maybe even go insane...

How does one find their real smile again?

Is it deep inside the heart?
That thing pumping our blood
From our last breath back to our start

And if a real smile lives there
Deep inside our hearts...

Maybe we were always smiling

Even when we're covered in the dirt of life

Because a real smile...
Never leaves

A real smile never thieves
A real smile always gives

So maybe a real smile...
Is as easy as connecting the dots

Because a real smile...
Smiles regardless of thoughts

So farewell restless mind
It's no longer your time

Now is the moment
Our heart steps up to do the grind

POEM 7: JULY 25, 2024
"Crime"

*A rotting tree aches with sorrow For
the hollowness that's in your eyes*

*The starving bird who cries no more
While it twists and turns as it flies*

POEM 5: MARCH 14, 2024
"Star Angels"

To everyone looking at stars on stage…

I'm looking at you

There's a star inside you too

One of the most dangerous things you can do

Is compare yourself to others

Because that face of yours

That face right there…

Is perfect

It doesn't need a stage

When a stage isn't there

Or when it only hurts to care

To know this world is in spiritual warfare

So when you're looking at a star on stage

Afterwards, go look in the mirror

And you'll begin to see clearer

There's a star there too…

Because God has a plan for each and every one of you

And whatever that plan is…

That face of yours

That face right there...

Was created to shine

And will stand the test of time

No matter what color

No matter what age

God loves us all the same

And we're all here just to play a lil game

The game called life

And even when it cuts deep, like a knife

We carry on to find

That life is beautiful

Even when it's not

And life is worth it

Even when it's fire burns too hot

So keep on shining star angel

Because you, your life

At every angle

Brightens up this dark place

Don't ever forget...

This world needs... your beautiful face

The withered croak of a diseased lagoon
Surrounds your soul as you shadow a moon

You ruthless criminal
Who tries to steal our time
And dull our shine

And fill our world with such hate and crime

Hoping to make us stumble
On our path up the climb

Yes the ground may rumble

As you feed your selfish greed
Using that trick up your sleeve

Gathering an army of spoiled ghouls
Aiming to turn lovers into fools

There's a monster inside lurking under the water
And inside the bodies of those who couldn't seem smarter

Who only charter
To their next barter
Betraying what it means to work harder

I don't feel bad for you
Because you chose evil

I don't feel sad for you
Because you choose to steal

When you lay your head down at night
And see the holy stars burn bright

You know you're wrong
And you know we're strong

Stronger than you
Because we stayed true

True to ourselves
True to the light
That brightens up the darkest of night
Even when life squeezes too tight

Yes even broken
We rise

Even injured
Above all cries
Above all lies
We own the skies

And leave you down
Behind
In the dust
Rotting away in toxic molten rust

Lies, violence and crime will grow dimmer starting now

And the time is coming when you'll see how

Xo,

Tessa

Circling back to our **HONOR** *example —*

After uploading this evidence, HONOR would likely begin to calculate a Crime Tax amount (which is previously voted on by you, Congress and The People). After this is calculated, a Case Report along with an initial Crime Tax Bill would be immediately sent to the NY Post were they are now allotted 30 days to provide acceptable evidence to dispute the offenses. Meanwhile, the Crime Tax Fine is immediately deducted from their Business Ethics Insurance Account (that we require all businesses to obtain in order to operate in The United States of America), the Article is flagged publicly, pending a final review of its illegal content. All of this would essentially be instantaneous and I would then save this HONOR Case as a template in the App and repeat it for the other news outlets who committed similar offenses.

As we polish out the details here Mr. President, what we have is technology that can provide us with an opportunity to radically reduce the amount of crime that is polluting this nation. It is my duty as an American Citizen, and yours as President sir, to utilize these long trains of abuses and usurpations, pursuing invariably the same Object that evinced a design to reduce me under absolute Despotism and correct injustices at their root to best serve this country.

Whether we like it or not sir… it appears what we have here is an epidemic of media personnel abusing the Freedom of Speech to intentionally harm others. Defamation and false reporting is a crime… and a serious one. The impacts of these crimes can cause irreparable damage to people's careers, families and friends. These crimes essentially ruin or end lives …which is a felony, sir. We need to properly prosecute all acts of reckless and malicious news reporting where evidence is fabricated, altered or manipulated… simply to bully or harm others.

Harming other people is a criminal act… and doing so… simply to increase publication circulation… is a betrayal to the values of America

On top of this, we have news outlets electively not covering substantial news that is vital to the progression of society. As Americans, we deserve the right to access accurate intelligent information that will benefit our lives… not pollute our lives. We need to update the Constitution to regulate the media so the American People don't continue to suffer the consequences of yet another under-regulated, unruly industry. While we're at it— we should vote on the percentage of negative material being reported and consider establishing… in my opinion.. at least a 70 % to 30 % law on negative to positive content… because right now sir.. my guess is the percentage of news we are forced to consume daily is around 90% negative. This is literally toxic pollution to the spirit of America… and it feeds crime sir.

Oh, and by the way, Mr. President — when I finally made it to the first choice "jetliner" rental... come to believe it... the house belongs to the grandson of William Natcher. The only Congressman in the history of The United States who held a near perfect Voting Record. Mr. Natcher upheld a .04% absence record for the entirety of his service. I'll be even more bold to say Mr. Natcher should be a new benchmark for America sir.. for everyone who works for our Government. Oh, and you may be wondering why I'm still talking. Well, as it turns out, I'm a descendant of the 7th President of The United States — the only President in the history of our nation when America had zero debt... for the entirety of his term.

So, before we officially wrap this up Mr. President, since crimes in America are just overflowing in all directions... let's quickly revisit the Constitution. There may be a few loose ends that will tremendously improve this country once they are tightened up...

ITEM ONE

THE CONSTITUTION OF THE UNITED STATES OF AMERICA

Written in 1787, ratified in 1788, and in operation since 1789, the United States Constitution is the world's longest surviving written charter of government. Its first three words—"We The People"—affirm that the government of the United States exists to serve its citizens. The supremacy of the people through their elected representatives is recognized in Article I, which creates a Congress consisting of a Senate and a House of Representatives. The positioning of Congress at the beginning of the Constitution reaffirms its status as the "First Branch" of the federal government.

The Constitution assigned to Congress responsibility for organizing the executive and judicial branches, raising revenue, declaring war, and making all laws necessary for executing these powers. The president is permitted to veto specific legislative acts, but Congress has the authority to override presidential vetoes by two-thirds majorities of both houses. The Constitution also provides that the Senate advise and consent on key executive and judicial appointments and on the ratification of treaties.

For over two centuries the Constitution has remained in force because its framers successfully separated and balanced governmental powers to safeguard the interests of majority rule and minority rights, of liberty and equality, and of the central and state governments. More a concise statement of national principles than a detailed plan of governmental operation, the Constitution has evolved to meet the changing needs of a modern society profoundly different from the eighteenth-century world in which its creators lived.

*SUGGESTED ADDITION — UPON WHICH THE PROGRESSION OF UNRULY SYSTEMIC BODIES FORCES THE SUPREMACY OF THE PEOPLE TOWARD AN INJUSTICE SYSTEM, THE CONSTITUTION EVOLVES TO INCLUDE MORE DETAILED PLANS OF GOVERNMENTAL OPERATIONS SO THAT IT MAY BEST PRESERVE THE PEACE AND SANCTITY OF THE UNITED STATES.

ITEM TWO
AMENDMENTS TO THE CONSTITUTION

Amendment I (1791)

Congress shall make no law respecting an establishment of religion, or prohibiting the free exercise thereof; or abridging the freedom of speech, or of the press; or the right of the people peaceably to assemble, and to petition the Government for a redress of grievances.

*SUGGESTED ADDITION — FREEDOM OF LICIT SPEECH OR OF THE ETHICAL PRESS,

The first ten amendments comprise the Bill of Rights. The first amendment protects religious freedom by prohibiting the establishment of an official or exclusive church or sect. Free speech and free press are protected, although they can be limited for reasons of defamation, obscenity, and certain forms of state censorship, especially during wartime. The freedom of assembly and petition also covers marching, picketing and pamphleteering.

Amendment II (1791)

A well regulated Militia, being necessary to the security of a free State, the right of the people to keep and bear Arms, shall not be infringed.

Whether this provision protects the individual's right to own firearms or whether it deals only with the collective right of the people to arm and maintain a militia is strongly debated.

Amendment III (1791)

No Soldier shall, in time of peace be quartered in any house, without the consent of the Owner, nor in time of war, but in a manner to be prescribed by law.

This virtually obsolete provision was in response to anger over the British military practice of quartering soldiers in colonists' homes.

ITEM THREE

CONSTITUTION OF THE UNITED STATES

In all Cases affecting Ambassadors, other public Ministers and Consuls, and those in which a State shall be Party, the supreme Court shall have original Jurisdiction. In all the other Cases before mentioned, the supreme Court shall have appellate Jurisdiction, both as to Law and Fact, with such Exceptions, and under such Regulations as the Congress shall make.

Certain cases may be brought directly to the Supreme Court without having been heard by another court. Under statute, the Supreme Court also exercises appellate review, that is the right to review the decisions of a lower federal or state court.

*SUGGESTED ADDITION — "THE TRIAL OF ALL QUALIFYING CRIMES, EXCEPT IN...

The Trial of all Crimes, except in Cases of Impeachment, shall be by Jury; and such Trial shall be held in the State where the said Crimes shall have been committed; but when not committed within any State, the Trial shall be at such Place or Places as the Congress may by Law have directed.

Anyone accused of a crime has a right to a trial by jury, except in the case of impeachments. This right was further defined and strengthened by the 6th, 7th, 8th, and 9th amendments.

Section 3. Treason against the United States, shall consist only in levying War against them, or in adhering to their Enemies, giving them Aid and Comfort. No Person shall be convicted of Treason unless on the Testimony of two Witnesses to the same overt Act, or on Confession in open Court.

The Congress shall have Power to declare the Punishment of Treason, but no Attainder of Treason shall work Corruption of Blood, or Forfeiture except during the Life of the Person attainted.

This clause limits Congress' ability to define treason or to set its punishment, as a means of preventing political "offenders" from being charged as traitors. At least two witnesses must testify in court that the defendant committed a treasonable act.

ITEM FOUR

Amendment IV (1791)

The right of the people to be secure in their persons, houses, papers, and effects, against unreasonable searches and seizures, shall not be violated, and no Warrants shall issue, but upon probable cause, supported by Oath or affirmation, and particularly describing the place to be searched, and the persons or things to be seized.

Applying to arrests and to searches of persons, homes, and other private places, this amendment requires a warrant, thereby placing a neutral magistrate between the police and the citizen.

Amendment V (1791)

No person shall be held to answer for a capital, or otherwise infamous crime, unless on a presentment or indictment of a Grand Jury, except in cases arising in the land or naval forces, or in the Militia, when in actual service in time of War or public danger; nor shall any person be subject for the same offence to be twice put in jeopardy of life or limb; nor shall be compelled in any criminal case to be a witness against himself, nor be deprived of life, liberty, or property, without due process of law; nor shall private property be taken for public use, without just compensation.

Indictment by a grand jury requires the decision of ordinary citizens to place one in danger of conviction. Double jeopardy means that when one has been convicted or acquitted, the government cannot place that person on trial again. The self-incrimination clause means that the prosecution must establish guilt by independent evidence and not by extorting a confession from the suspect, although voluntary confessions are not precluded. Due process of the law requires the government to observe proper and traditional methods in depriving one of an important right. Finally, when the government seizes property to use in the public interest, it must pay the owner fair value.

* SUGGESTED REMOVAL — "SHALL NOR BE COMPELLED IN ANY CRIMINAL CASE TO BE A WITNESS AGAINST HIMSELF."

REASON: A NEUTRAL, OBJECTIVE TESTIMONY FROM A SUSPECT IS ESSENTIAL TO INVESTIGATION.

ITEM FIVE

CONSTITUTION OF THE UNITED STATES

*SUGGESTED CORRECTION — "IN QUALIFYING CRIMINAL PROSECUTIONS, THE ACCUSED SHALL ENJOY.."

Amendment VI (1791)

In all criminal prosecutions, the accused shall enjoy the right to a speedy and public trial, by an impartial jury of the State and district wherein the crime shall have been committed, which district shall have been previously ascertained by law, and to be informed of the nature and cause of the accusation; to be confronted with the witnesses against him; to have compulsory process for obtaining witnesses in his favor, and to have the Assistance of Counsel for his defence.

Defendants in criminal cases are entitled to public trials that follow relatively soon after initiation of the charges. Witnesses must be brought to the trial to testify before the defendant, judge, and jury. Defendants are also entitled to compel witnesses on their behalf to appear and testify.

*SUGGESTED ADDITION — "THE REMAINING CRIMINAL PROSECUTIONS SHALL BE TAXED ACCORDINGLY AND PROCESSED IN A SPEEDY MANNER USING THE LATEST METHODS OF DEFENDING THE PEACE."

Amendment VII (1791)

In Suits at common law, where the value in controversy shall exceed twenty dollars, the right of trial by jury shall be preserved, and no fact tried by a jury, shall be otherwise re-examined in any Court of the United States, than according to the rules of the common law.

Mistrustful of judges, the people insisted on the right to jury trial in civil cases. The minimum level, $20, is so low today that it would burden the federal judiciary, so various devices have been developed to permit alternative resolution of disputes.

*SUGGESTED ADDITION — "THE RIGHT OF TRIAL BY JURY SHALL BE PRESERVED FOR QUALIFYING CASES, AND NO FACT..."

Amendment VIII (1791)

Excessive bail shall not be required, nor excessive fines imposed, nor cruel and unusual punishments inflicted.

Neither bail nor punishment for a crime are to be unreasonably severe. The "cruel and unusual punishments" clause has been the basis for challenges to the death penalty.

ITEM SIX

person having the greatest number of votes as Vice-President, shall be the Vice-President, if such number be a majority of the whole number of Electors appointed, and if no person have a majority, then from the two highest numbers on the list, the Senate shall choose the Vice-President; a quorum for the purpose shall consist of two-thirds of the whole number of Senators, and a majority of the whole number shall be necessary to a choice. But no person constitutionally ineligible to the office of President shall be eligible to that of Vice-President of the United States.

After the disputed election of 1800, this amendment required separate designation of presidential and vice presidential candidates, each of whom must meet the same qualifications for eligibility as the president.

Amendment XIII (1865)

*Suggested Addition —
"Neither slavery, involuntary servitude, except as punishment for crime whereof the party shall have been duly convicted, nor oppression, organizational or otherwise, shall exist."

Section 1. Neither slavery nor involuntary servitude, except as a punishment for crime whereof the party shall have been duly convicted, shall exist within the United States, or any place subject to their jurisdiction.

Section 2. Congress shall have power to enforce this article by appropriate legislation.

President Lincoln's Emancipation Proclamation did not apply to slavery in the states that had not seceded. To abolish slavery entirely, Congress proposed this amendment, which also gave Congress specific authority to enforce the amendment by legislation. Under these provisions, Congress has legislated against slavery-like conditions, such as peonage.

Amendment XIV (1868)

Section 1. All persons born or naturalized in the United States and subject to the jurisdiction thereof, are citizens of the United States and of the State wherein they reside. No State shall make or enforce any law which shall

In the *Dred Scott* decision of 1857, the Supreme Court had said that African-Americans were not citizens. This amendment declared that every person born or naturalized in the U.S. was a citizen. The amendment's "due process" clause has had enormous

ITEM SEVEN

*SUGGESTED ADJUSTMENT —
"SHALL NOT BE QUESTIONED."
   CHANGE TO —>
"SHALL BE DIRECTLY REDUCED BY DULY PROCESSED CRIME TAX FINES AND QUALIFYING DEBT AMOUNTS ARE TO BE SHARED IN AN ANNUAL FISCAL REPORT MADE AVAILABLE TO ALL TAX PAYING CITIZENS."

AMENDMENT XIV

office, civil or military, under the United States, or under any State, who, having previously taken an oath, as a member of Congress, or as an officer of the United States, or as a member of any State legislature, or as an executive or judicial officer of any State, to support the Constitution of the United States, shall have engaged in insurrection or rebellion against the same, or given aid or comfort to the enemies thereof. But Congress may by a vote of two-thirds of each House, remove such disability.

Section 4. The validity of the public debt of the United States, authorized by law, including debts incurred for payment of pensions and bounties for services in suppressing insurrection or rebellion, shall not be questioned. But neither the United States nor any State shall assume or pay any debt or obligation incurred in aid of insurrection or rebellion against the United States, or any claim for the loss or emancipation of any slave; but all such debts, obligations and claims shall be held illegal and void.

Section 5. The Congress shall have power to enforce, by appropriate legislation, the provisions of this article.

ITEM EIGHT

ARTICLE I

No Capitation, or other direct, Tax shall be laid, unless in Proportion to the Census of Enumeration herein before directed to be taken.

Direct taxes are poll or "head" taxes and taxes on land. The Supreme Court once held that income taxes were unconstitutional direct taxes, a result overturned by the 16th amendment.

No Tax or Duty shall be laid on Articles exported from any State.

To prohibit discrimination against any states or regions, Congress cannot tax goods exported from a state to foreign countries or those that move between states.

No Preference shall be given by any Regulation of Commerce or Revenue to the Ports of one State over those of another: nor shall Vessels bound to, or from, one State, be obliged to enter, clear or pay Duties in another.

Congress cannot favor one state against another while regulating trade.

*SUGGESTED ADJUSTMENT — "SHALL BE PUBLISHED FROM TIME TO TIME.

CHANGE TO —>

"SHALL BE MADE AVAILABLE TO ALL TAX PAYING CITIZENS TWICE ANNUALLY AND PUBLISHED FROM TIME TO TIME."

No Money shall be drawn from the Treasury, but in Consequence of Appropriations made by Law; and a regular Statement and Account of the Receipts and Expenditures of all public Money shall be published from time to time.

The departments and agencies of the executive branch may not spend any money that Congress has not appropriated, or use federal money for any purpose that Congress has not specified.

No Title of Nobility shall be granted by the United States: And no Person holding any Office of Profit or Trust under them, shall, without the Consent of the Congress, accept of any present, Emolument, Office, or Title, of any kind whatever, from any King, Prince or foreign State.

This clause was designed to end the aristocratic tendencies that the American Revolution had been fought against. Federal officials must turn over to the government all but minimal gifts from foreign nations.

ITEM NINE

CONSTITUTION OF THE UNITED STATES

Section 9. *The Migration or Importation of such Persons as any of the States now existing shall think proper to admit, shall not be prohibited by the Congress prior to the Year one thousand eight hundred and eight, but a Tax or duty may be imposed on such Importation, not exceeding ten dollars for each Person.*

This obsolete provision was designed to protect the slave trade from congressional restriction for a period of time.

The Privilege of the Writ of Habeas Corpus shall not be suspended, unless when in Cases of Rebellion or Invasion the public Safety may require it.

*SUGGESTED ADJUSTMENT — "SHALL APPLY TO QUALIFYING CRIMINAL PROSECUTIONS."

*OTHERWISE SUGGESTING THE PASSING OF THESE LAWS

No Bill of Attainder or ex post facto Law shall be passed.

REASON: WE HAVE AN OVERWHELMING AMOUNT OF CRIMES AND NEED TO BEGIN PROCESSING THEM QUICKLY — SPECIFICALLY IN REGARDS TO EXECUTING A CRIMINAL TAX LAW AND UTILIZING CRIME TAX FINES TO PAY OFF AMERICA'S DEBT.

Habeas corpus is a judicial device by which jailed people may require their jailer to justify their imprisonment to a court. It is a fundamental safeguard of individual liberty, and the Supreme Court has interpreted it to give federal courts review over state court convictions and to enforce federal constitutional guarantees. It is generally accepted that only Congress has the power to suspend *habeas corpus*. President Abraham Lincoln's suspension of the right during the Civil War met with strong opposition.

A bill of attainder is a legislative act declaring the guilt of an individual or a group of persons and punishing them. Only the courts may determine whether one has violated a criminal statute. An *ex post facto* law declares an act illegal after it has been committed, or increases the punishment for an offense already committed.

ITEM TEN

Every Order, Resolution, or Vote to which the Concurrence of the Senate and House of Representatives may be necessary (except on a question of Adjournment) shall be presented to the President of the United States; and before the Same shall take Effect, shall be approved by him, or being disapproved by him, shall be repassed by two thirds of the Senate and House of Representatives, according to the Rules and Limitations prescribed in the Case of a Bill.

This clause prevents Congress from circumventing the previous clause by calling a bill something else. All it means is that any "order, resolution, or vote" that has the force of law must be passed in the manner of a bill.

Section 8. The Congress shall have Power To lay and collect Taxes, Duties, Imposts and Excises, to pay the Debts and provide for the common Defence and general Welfare of the United States; but all Duties, Imposts and Excises shall be uniform throughout the United States;

Section 8 begins the enumerated powers of the federal government delegated to Congress. The first is the power to tax and to spend the money raised by taxes, to provide for the nation's defense and general welfare. This section was supplemented by the 16th amendment, which permitted Congress to levy an income tax.

To borrow Money on the credit of the United States;

*SUGGESTED ADDITION — "AND A REGULAR STATEMENT AND ACCOUNT OF THE RECEIPTS AND EXPENDITURES OF ALL BORROWED MONEY SHALL BE MADE AVAILABLE TO ALL TAX PAYING CITIZENS TWICE ANNUALLY."

Congress can borrow money through the issuance of bonds and other means. When it borrows money, the United States creates a binding obligation to repay the debt and cannot repudiate it.

REASON: THIS WILL REDUCE OUR DEBT BY ENCOURAGING THE UTILIZATION OF LUCRATIVE RESOURCES TO FULFILL CAUSES AND DUTIES BEFORE ADDING TO OUR DEBT.

ITEM ELEVEN

*SUGGESTED ADDITION — "ALL MEMBERS OF BOTH SENATE AND HOUSE MUST HOLD A MINIMUM OF A 70% ATTENDANCE VOTING RECORD FOR THE DURATION OF THEIR TERM. IF ADDITIONAL ABSENCES OCCUR, THEIR SEAT IS AUTOMATICALLY FORFEITED TO THE NEXT ELIGIBLE MEMBER.

REASON: THE SOLE JOB OF A MEMBER OF CONGRESS IS TO VOTE ON LEGISLATURE. FREQUENT ABSENCES AREA A CONTRACTUAL BREACH OF DUTY.

Section 5. Each House shall be the Judge of the Elections, Returns and Qualifications of its own Members, and a Majority of each shall constitute a Quorum to do Business; but a smaller Number may adjourn from day to day, and may be authorized to compel the Attendance of absent Members, in such Manner, and under such Penalties as each House may provide.

Each House may determine the Rules of its Proceedings, punish its Members for disorderly Behaviour, and, with the Concurrence of two thirds, expel a Member.

Each House shall keep a Journal of its Proceedings, and from time to time publish the same, excepting such Parts as may in their Judgment require Secrecy; and the Yeas and Nays of the Members of either House on any question shall, at the Desire of one fifth of those Present, be entered on the Journal.

Neither House, during the Session of Congress, shall, without the Consent of the other, adjourn for more than three days, nor to any other Place than that in which the two Houses shall be sitting.

The House and Senate decide whether their members are qualified to serve and have been properly elected, and determine any disputed elections. One-half plus one of each house is necessary to make a quorum to conduct business.

The Senate and House each sets its own rules, disciplines its own members, and by a two-thirds vote can expel a member. Censure and lesser punishments require only a majority vote.

The Senate and House each publish journals listing bills passed, amendments offered, motions made, and votes taken. In addition to these journals, Congress publishes an essentially verbatim account of its debates, called the *Congressional Record*. Videotapes of floor proceedings are deposited at the National Archives.

This section was included to prevent either chamber from blocking legislation through its refusal to meet. Each chamber takes very seriously its independence of the other body. To avoid having to ask the other chamber for permission to adjourn, the Senate and House simply conduct *pro forma* (as a matter of form) sessions to meet the three-day constitutional requirement. No business is conducted at these sessions, which generally last for less than one minute.

ITEM TWELVE

ARTICLE I

Every Bill which shall have passed the House of Representatives and the Senate, shall, before it become a law, be presented to the President of the United States: If he approve he shall sign it, but if not he shall return it, with his Objections to that House in which it shall have originated, who shall enter the Objections at large on their Journal, and proceed to reconsider it. If after such Reconsideration two thirds of that House shall agree to pass the Bill, it shall be sent, together with the Objections, to the other House, by which it shall likewise be reconsidered, and if approved by two thirds of that House, it shall become a Law. But in all such Cases the Votes of both Houses shall be determined by Yeas and Nays, and the Names of the Persons voting for and against the Bill shall be entered on the Journal of each House respectively. If any Bill shall not be returned by the President within ten Days (Sundays excepted) after it shall have been presented to him, the Same shall be a Law, in like Manner as if he had signed it, unless the Congress by their Adjournment prevent its Return, in which Case it shall not be a Law.

The "presentment clause" describes the *only* way that a bill can become law: it must be passed in identical form by both Houses and it must be signed by the president or passed by a two-thirds vote of Congress over the president's veto. If, while Congress is in session, the president does not sign a bill, it automatically becomes law. If Congress has adjourned or is in recess, the president can "pocket veto" the bill—in a sense, simply putting it in his pocket, unsigned. Congress cannot override bills that have been pocket vetoed.

*SUGGESTED ADJUSTMENT — "UNLESS THE CONGRESS BY THEIR ADJOURNMENT PREVENTS ITS RETURN, IN WHICH CASE IT SHALL NOT BE A LAW."

CHANGE TO —>
"UNLESS THE CONGRESS BY THEIR ADJOURNMENT PREVENTS ITS RETURN, IN WHICH CASE IT SHALL BE TURNED INTO A DESIGNATED AGENT ASSIGNED TO RECEIVING PRESIDENT MESSAGES DURING AN ADJOURNMENT."

REASON: TO PROTECT AGAINST LEGAL AMBIGUITY, REDUCE TENSION BETWEEN BRANCHES, PREVENT THE INVALIDATION OF LEGISLATION AND SAVE TIME.. THUS REDUCING UNNECESSARY DEBT AND EXPENDITURES.

ARTICLE I

ITEM THIRTEEN

*SUGGESTED ADJUSTMENT — "EACH HOUSE SHALL KEEP A JOURNAL OF ITS PROCEEDINGS AND FROM TIME TO TIME PUBLISH THE SAME"

CHANGE TO →

"EACH HOUSE SHALL KEEP A JOURNAL OF ITS PROCEEDINGS AND PUBLISH THEM WEEKLY ON THE UNITED STATES APP, ACCESSIBLE ONLY TO TAX PAYING CITIZENS, EXCEPTING SUCH PARTS AS MAY IN THEIR JUDGMENT REQUIRE SECRECY"

Section 5. Each House shall be the Judge of the Elections, Returns and Qualifications of its own Members, and a Majority of each shall constitute a Quorum to do Business; but a smaller Number may adjourn from day to day, and may be authorized to compel the Attendance of absent Members, in such Manner, and under such Penalties as each House may provide.

Each House may determine the Rules of its Proceedings, punish its Members for disorderly Behaviour, and, with the Concurrence of two thirds, expel a Member.

Each House shall keep a Journal of its Proceedings, and from time to time publish the same, excepting such Parts as may in their Judgment require Secrecy; and the Yeas and Nays of the Members of either House on any question shall, at the Desire of one fifth of those Present, be entered on the Journal.

Neither House, during the Session of Congress, shall, without the Consent of the other, adjourn for more than three days, nor to any other Place than that in which the two Houses shall be sitting.

The House and Senate decide whether their members are qualified to serve and have been properly elected, and determine any disputed elections. One-half plus one of each house is necessary to make a quorum to conduct business.

The Senate and House each sets its own rules, disciplines its own members, and by a two-thirds vote can expel a member. Censure and lesser punishments require only a majority vote.

The Senate and House each publish journals listing bills passed, amendments offered, motions made, and votes taken. In addition to these journals, Congress publishes an essentially verbatim account of its debates, called the *Congressional Record*. Videotapes of floor proceedings are deposited at the National Archives.

This section was included to prevent either chamber from blocking legislation through its refusal to meet. Each chamber takes very seriously its independence of the other body. To avoid having to ask the other chamber for permission to adjourn, the Senate and House simply conduct *pro forma* (as a matter of form) sessions to meet the three-day constitutional requirement. No business is conducted at these sessions, which generally last for less than one minute.

ITEM FOURTEEN

The Senate shall have the sole Power to try all Impeachments. When sitting for that Purpose, they shall be on Oath or Affirmation. When the President of the United States is tried the Chief Justice shall preside: And no Person shall be convicted without the Concurrence of two thirds of the Members present.

Judgment in Cases of Impeachment shall not extend further than to removal from Office, and disqualification to hold and enjoy any Office of honor, Trust or Profit under the United States: but the Party convicted shall nevertheless be liable and subject to Indictment, Trial, Judgment and Punishment, according to Law.

Section 4. The Times, Places and Manner of holding Elections for Senators and Representatives, shall be prescribed in each State by the Legislature thereof; but the Congress may at any time by Law make or alter such Regulations, except as to the Places of chusing Senators.

The Congress shall assemble at least once in every Year, and such Meeting shall *be on the first Monday in December*, unless they shall by Law appoint a different Day.

Once the House votes to impeach, the Senate conducts a trial to determine whether to convict or acquit. A two-thirds vote is necessary to remove the individual from office. The chief justice of the Supreme Court presides over the impeachment trial of a president.

Convicted persons can be barred from holding future office, and may be subject to criminal trial in the courts.

*SUGGESTED ADJUSTMENT —
"THE CONGRESS SHALL ASSEMBLE AT LEAST ONCE IN EVERY YEAR, AND SUCH MEETING..."
CHANGE TO —>
"THE CONGRESS SHALL ASSEMBLE AT LEAST THREE TIMES A YEAR"

Federal elections are conducted by the individual states, although Congress has gradually enacted laws that regulate those elections. The 17th amendment made the treatment of the election of senators and representatives the same.

The 20th amendment changed this provision for the convening of Congress from the first Monday in December to the 3rd of January.

REASON: FIRST MEETING IS INTRODUCTORY / ESTABLISHES ANNUAL GOALS. SECOND MEETING CHECKS STATUS TO MAKE ADJUSTMENTS AS NECESSARY. FINAL MEETING DETERMINES A HIT OR MISS OF ANNUAL GOALS.

ITEM FIFTEEN

CONSTITUTION OF THE UNITED STATES

We the People of the United States, in Order to form a more perfect Union, establish Justice, insure domestic Tranquillity, provide for the common defence, promote the general Welfare, and secure the Blessings of Liberty to ourselves and our Posterity, do ordain and establish this Constitution for the United States of America.

The Preamble explains the purposes of the Constitution, and defines the powers of the new government as originating from the people of the United States.

Article I

Section 1. All legislative Powers herein granted shall be vested in a Congress of the United States, which shall consist of a Senate and House of Representatives.

The Constitution divides the federal government into three branches, giving legislative powers to a bicameral (two chamber) Congress.

Section 2. The House of Representatives shall be composed of Members chosen every second Year by the People of the several States, and the Electors in each State shall have the Qualifications requisite for Electors of the most numerous Branch of the State Legislature.

The House of Representatives was intended to be "the people's house." Its members were elected directly by the voters in the states, and the entire House would have to stand for election every two years.

*SUGGESTED ADJUSTMENT — "...CHOSEN EVERY SECOND YEAR BY THE PEOPLE OF THE SEVERAL STATES..."
CHANGE TO —>
"...CHOSEN EVERY THIRD YEAR BY THE PEOPLE OF THE SEVERAL STATES..."

REASON: THE FIRST YEAR WARMS UP THE MEMBER FOR THEIR TERM. THE SECOND YEAR PROVIDES THEM AN OPPORTUNITY TO ADJUST AND IMPROVE TO REACH HIGHEST POTENTIAL. THIRD YEAR ENABLES MEMBER TO FUNCTION AS HIGHEST POTENTIAL AND PREPARE FOR RE-ELECTION OR RETIREMENT.

Also, Mr. President, now that this engine is warmed up, I'll toss you a few more ideas off the top of my head on how we can...

RESTORE AMERICA

You're a good catch aren't you, sir? A three sport athlete at the New York Military Academy I believe? Maybe we can address fixing America like a sport. In fact, I'd love to see profiles created for all Members of Congress on a new United States App. You know how we do it for athletes on TV before sporting events? I bet The People will agree... let's get to know who we are voting for and who's fightin' the good fight to keep America AMERICAN!

Here they are.. comin' straight at ya Mr. President. CATCH –

1. We create a United States App that will include (these features and more):

    A) An Advanced Security Feature: With a Certified Safe Seal to guarantee device privacy and provide Citizens with a service to scan their device and expose any Apps with fine print that spy on their device without permission.

    B) Laws (State and Federal): A comprehensive list of all state and federal laws. Note on this: Most people don't have easy access to laws and have no idea what they are. How can we expect there to be law and order in our country if we don't give The People an easily accessible blueprint.

    C) Health Section: disease prevention, vitality maintenance, expert tips, latest medical discoveries, recovery protocols, symptom checker, medicine facts and warning labels, list of all medicines and pharmaceutical companies, all registered doctors with reviews, nutritional information, etc.

    D) Life Skills Section: emotional coping techniques, communication strategies, budget training, etc.

    E) Spiritual Section: We don't enforce a religion. Instead we — educate Citizens on all the options available so they have healthy spiritual hygiene. In fact... if you recall our first President, George Washington... stated in his farewell address: "Of all the dispositions and habits which lead to political prosperity, Religion and morality are indispensable *supports*." 1

Mr. Washington questioned the patriotism of anyone who; "*should labour to subvert these great Pillars of human happiness, these firmest props of the duties of Men & citizens.*"

Our first President even argued that religion is vital to morality: *"Reason and experience both forbid us to expect that National morality can prevail in exclusion of religious principle,"* and that morality, in turn, *is an indispensable ingredient for a thriving democratic republic: "Tis substantially true, that virtue or morality is a necessary spring of popular government. The rule indeed extends with more or less force to every species of Free Government."*

Our second President, John Adams, agreed: *"It is religion and morality alone which can establish the principles upon which freedom can securely stand."* 2 In fact, without that firm foundation, our constitutional form of government would be in jeopardy:

> *"We have no government armed with power capable of contending with human passions unbridled by morality and religion. Our Constitution was made only for a moral people. It is wholly inadequate to the government of any other."* 3) 4

F) Admin Section — This would be a hub for taxes, legal documents, citizenship paperwork. We would outsource secure links to additional official sites and increase user identity protection by expanding document access to multiple servers.

G) Finance Section — This would include stock market training, access, budgeting courses, loans, credit card training, donation and fundraising opportunities, etc.

H) Safety Section — This would include natural disaster training, law enforcement protocols and resources, driver's license renewal training, safe gun use training, self defense courses, witness protection resources, additional crime reporting, etc.

I) State and National Events and Holidays Section — self explanatory

J) A "Helping Hand" Section — This is similar to the function of a non-profit except it's cleaner and faster. We create a system for people recovering from natural disasters or crimes to sign up and receive direct help from other Americans.

Donations can be made to collective groups or straight to individuals/families in need at the donor's choice and we'll execute it using existing financial portals such as PayPal, Venmo or Zelle, etc.

2. We send out an Annual Bulletin on Tax Day to update Citizens on America's financial status. We let everyone know how we did that year… are we improving crime rates, death rates, where are we with various problems in the country, what are the problems in our country, what is the status of our natural resources, parks, climate change, etc. On this bulletin we spotlight that year's achievements of exemplary Citizens, Members of Congress, Companies and Organizations. Think of this kind of like a "yearbook" for America.

   A) In addition to the above, we facilitate a T-shirt program where all taxpaying Citizens can digitally create and upload a custom T-Shirt design to select and receive upon the completion of their Tax Return. They can either have the shirt shipped to them to keep or donate it to a non-tax paying Citizen who has signed up for the program. Children can upload designs too. Imagine someone living in Florida wearing a t-shirt designed by someone living in Idaho or vice versa. It's subtle, fun and will promote feelings of unity.

3. We require all hospitals to send first-time parents home with a "Parenting Tool Kit" at child birth. A lot of the issues causing homelessness and increased crime today such as addictions, mental illness, disorderly conduct, etc can be prevented during adolescence using proper parenting techniques. The Parenting Tool Kit can include a variety of expert-backed styles so parents choose the style that suits them best.

4. For crimes committed by under-age Americans, we begin including punishment for the parents. This is similar to Thailand which is home to one of the world's safest communities.

5. We provide Citizens with an all-inclusive archive of music and movies and revive Blockbuster (or a company similar) to ship DVDs. In case of power outages, internet service or subscription issues… Citizens should not lose access to movies. They should also be able to educate themselves on all the movies released over the years. This platform can be both a source of reference information as well as a place to purchase physical TVs, DVDs and DVD players. We do the same thing with music (CDs, CD players, Vinyls, etc) Art is essential to the mental, emotional and spiritual health of humanity and should be respected as such.

6. According to recent studies, there is one suicide every 11 minutes and the majority of these deaths are people age 15-29. This age group often struggles with healthy social media use so let's require a Warning Disclaimer to pop up upon the opening of a Social Media App. Anything that has been proven to be highly addictive or dangerous… cigarettes, alcohol, drugs, etc… informs the user of the high risk of developing addiction along with recommended safety tips. Social media is no different because it's already causing an epidemic of teen mental illness and suicide.

7. Outlaw the purchase of social media followers, comments, reviews.. and implement Crime Tax fines for violators. This will improve the integrity of society and our economy.

8. For "Influencers" who claim to be experts in a particular field, we require they list their training, licenses and credentials on their profile. Note on this: there is a trend of young adults listening to "online influencers" more than their teachers and professors. We need to confirm people educating the future of America actually know what they claim to know.

9. Outlaw internet browsers from violating people's social media post settings.

10. Establish moral groundwork for all reporters, journalists and news outlets to follow and polish license requirements. Criminally prosecute reporters and journalists who intentionally harm others through means of intentionally fabricating or manipulating information to publish false, biased or uneducated statements as truth.

11. Require all states to have driver's retake an online safety test once per year during vehicle registration renewal — reduce the test to 30 minutes.

12. Public school programs — we need nationwide reform on this. Certain schools have fallen behind and are forgetting to require students to say the Pledge of Allegiance. Note: I have more detailed ideas on this to discuss.

13. Cap weekly mediations for personal injury attorneys and require a minimum of 30 minute case review prior to all mediation start with optional recording and AI ethics monitoring for the entirety of the mediation at the discretion of the plaintiff to ensure ethical handling.

14. Research and outlaw toxins from clothing that have already been outlawed in other countries.

15. Include building safety checks for all fire stations and police stations. These buildings must be in compliance with current standards safety and health conditions.

16. Update hours, salaries and training for all policemen to ensure nationwide structure, clarity on protocol, access to the latest tools, etc.

17. Establish and provide mental health protocols for firefighters, soldiers and policemen.. Example: regular EMDR or hypnotherapy, pet foster program, elective hobby education and resources, etc. Our first responders have an alarming suicide rate due being forced to experience "on-the-job" trauma. If they protect us... we protect them. And we can do this by implementing trauma prevention, recovery and management protocols... nationwide.

Phew, on that note... I need to take a break.

More ideas to come...

That's all for now Mr. President. OVER AND OUT!

WHAT DO YOU THINK?

Let's continue the conversation...

References:

1) From The Farewell Address: Transcript of the Final Manuscript, 20 in The Papers of George Washington collected by the University of Virginia as found at http://gwpapers.virginia.edu/documents/farewell/transcript.html. 74
2) John Adams to Zabdiel Adams, June 21, 1776 in Charles Francis Adams, ed., The Works of John Adams - Second President of the United States: with a Life of the Author, Notes, and Illustration, 10 vols., (Boston: Little, Brown, & Co., 1854), 9:401.
3) John Adams to the officers of the First Brigade of the Third Division of the Militia of Massachusetts on October 11, 1798 as found in Adams, Works of John Adams, 9:228-229.
4) Dr. Kenyn Cureton "The Ten Commandments: Foundation of American Society" Item Code BL10D01 as found at https://downloads.frc.org/EF/ EF10I86.pdf

SPECIAL THANKS

THE ONE AND THE ONLY

YOU KNOW WHO YOU ARE

About the Author

Tessa Lyn

Tessa is a family girl at heart with quite the rocky start...
pursuing world records as a rebel artist... to finding love as the
ultimate way of dreaming the hardest.

Overcoming any obstacle to find a way home… no matter how many demons may roam… on her quest to creating the best… family… home… and life… as a devoted Mom… as a supreme wife.

By age 3, Tessa was participating in dance, gymnastics and Girl Scouts; and frequently found herself winning city-wide coloring contests.

She spent the remainder of her childhood attending public schools and keeping active in soccer, theater, dance, choir, ice skating and yearbook. After completing film school at The University of Texas, Tessa studied 7 different acting techniques to one day create her own "secret sauce."

Shortly after moving to Hollywood, Tessa began booking leading roles in films like "The First Born" "Diamond" and "Death in the Abstract."

It didn't take long for Tessa's deeply rooted passion for cinema, and the invention of Apple's first smartphone with a 4K camera, to lead Tessa to become the first female to make a feature film on the iPhone.

With a competitive athlete background – Tessa hunted for the ultimate challenge and entered timed-filmmaking competitions to learn how to create under extreme pressure.

This higher level of pressure suited Tessa well as she began winning awards and accolades for every project she created as the star/writer/director. Driven to earn a spot in history books, Tessa set out to inspire audiences not only to overcome their fear but to go beyond their self-perceive limits.

TESSA CRAFTED THE FEATURE FILM CINEMA REBEL ESSENTIALLY BACKWARDS BY WEAVING TOGETHER SHORT FILMS SHE MADE IN 2017-2018 DURING HER TIME PIONEERING THE CINEMATIC CAPABILITIES OF AN IPHONE CAMERA

Tessa then retroactively crafted a plot to weave these films together and became drawn to the idea of bringing the craft of filmmaking to new heights for humankind and give audiences a theatrical experience they've never had before. To turn this dream into reality, Tessa committed to embodying Cinema Rebel's main character, Daisy Blaine, both in front of the camera and behind it...

In order to set the world record for the largest performance for a motion picture artist in history, Tessa spent 90% of her time offline inside a private production studio where she worked devotedly in solitude for 5 1/2 years - to learn and execute - all aspects of filmmaking from pre-production to production to post-production.

It was in these quiet moments that gradually turned into years.... frame by frame... pixel by pixel... Tessa discovered if she could make her dreams come true with simply the phone in her hand and her devotion to Christ

After a short festival circuit around the world, Cinema Rebel went on to receive 18 award wins/nominations and may have set up to 6 new world records for the craft of film...

> BIGGEST PERFORMANCE BY AN ACTRESS IN HOLLYWOOD, EVER
> THE LARGEST PERFORMANCE BY A MOTION PICTURE ARTIST IN HISTORY
> FIRST FEMALE DIRECTOR TO MAKE A FEATURE FILM ON THE IPHONE
> THE LONGEST PERFORMANCE BY A PERFORMER IN HOLLYWOOD
> MOST FILM CREDITS FOR THE SAME CREW MEMBER IN THE SAME FILM
> MOST DEBUTING AWARD WINS & NOMS FOR A FILM SHOT ON THE IPHONE
> FIRST LEAD ACTRESS TO STAR IN AND CREW THE SAME FEATURE FILM

Despite Cinema Rebel's global unprecedented achievements, the pioneering methods Tessa used in her innovative self-made approach prevented the film from initially being released to the public. Interestingly enough, in a strange convergence of torturous events, Tessa's life took an unforseen twist as she completed the final stages of post-production for Cinema Rebel which lead to her forced survival of the catastrophic crime webs outlined in this book.

In spite of the chronic chaos that comes along with one's foundation being shattered repeatedly Tessa remains an unbreakable vessel of light who reminds us that a real home isn't found in the walls surrounding you...rather in the deepest crevices of your heart.

www.ingramcontent.com/pod-product-compliance
Lightning Source LLC
Chambersburg PA
CBHW040733060526
44119CB00078B/289